The New
Brown Bag

Wipe the Tears

The New
Brown Bag

Wipe the Tears
30 Children's Sermons on Death

Phyllis Vos Wezeman
Anna L. Liechty
Kenneth R. Wezeman

THE
PILGRIM
PRESS
Cleveland

To Howard and Mary Uhrig . . .

. . . whose strong faith in the midst of sorrow is a testimony to the steadfast love of God.

—(P.V.W. & K.R.W.)

In memory of Sheryl Ann Liechty . . .

. . . whose fifteen years on earth left her family and friends with many lessons about the importance of living despite the reality of death.

—(A.L.L.)

The Pilgrim Press, 700 Prospect Avenue East, Cleveland, Ohio 44115-1100

© 2004 Phyllis Vos Wezeman, Anna L. Liechty, and Kenneth R. Wezeman

"Hymn of Promise," from *Hymn Stories for Children: Lent and Easter.* Copyright 2002. Adapted and used by permission of LOGOS System Associates.

"For All the Saints," from *Hymn Stories for Children: Special Days and Holidays.* Copyright 1994 by Phyllis Vos Wezeman and Anna L. Liechty. Reprinted by permission of the authors.

"Treasure Chest," from *Festival of Faith: A Vacation Church School Curriculum Celebrating the Gifts of God.* Copyright 1993 by Educational Ministries, Inc. Adapted and used by permission.

Library of Congress Cataloging-in-Publication Data

Wezeman, Phyllis Vos.
    Wipe the tears : 30 children's sermons on death / Phyllis Vos Wezeman,
    Anna L. Liechty, Kenneth R. Wezeman.
        p. cm. (The new brown bag)
    ISBN 0-8298-1520-1 (pbk. : alk. paper)
        1. Children's sermons. 2. Death—Religious aspects—Christianity—Juvenile
literature. I. Liechty, Anna L. II. Wezeman, Kenneth R. III. Title. IV. Series.

BV4315.W49   2003
252'.53—dc22

                                    2004044278

Contents

Introduction

Death is a topic we prefer to avoid; however, its reality surrounds us daily. We are indirectly affected when we read news reports of battle casualties in war or hear of traffic fatalities from automobile accidents. We follow accounts of murders in nearby communities or watch video coverage of natural disasters that claim innocent lives. In our own family circles, grandparents die after a lengthy illness or cancer claims a younger parent or sibling. Perhaps a heart attack takes a friend or neighbor unexpectedly. Even children's playmates fall victim to childhood diseases. Although death is one of life's certainties, we avoid the subject and prefer to distance ourselves and our children from its reality. However, if our only strategy for dealing with death's reality is avoidance, we deny ourselves and our children the opportunity of developing a faith that sustains us in the most difficult situations life brings.

Both Hebrew and Christian Scriptures have much to say to us on the subject of death. God's Word explains the coming of death as the consequence of sin; however, scripture also reveals that God immediately developed the plan for saving humankind. Prophets and psalmists offer words that alternately challenge and comfort us to embrace both the certainty of death and the hope of eternal life. Ultimately, Christ's resurrection brings victory over sin and death and gives believers the faith to see the end of life on earth as the beginning of new life with God.

While we do not welcome the lessons that come to us from facing loss or experiencing grief and pain, we do acknowledge that all of us must ultimately develop the tools to deal with "the valley of the shadow of death." The lessons contained in *Wipe the Tears: 30*

Children's Sermons on Death, are designed to enable participants to acknowledge and talk about the reality we try to deny. As you use this book to help others grapple with issues related to death, may you experience the reality of faith and together proclaim with Saint Paul the words of First Corinthians 15:57, "Thanks be to God, who gives us the victory through our Lord Jesus Christ."

Overview

What is this book?

Wipe the Tears: 30 Children's Sermons on Death is a collection of thirty messages primarily designed for kindergarten through upper-elementary youth. This resource addresses the subject of death from a variety of approaches. While each sermon is based on a scripture passage or verse, some lessons focus on biblical stories related to death, several explain contemporary and traditional hymns that address the topic, and others explore theological themes regarding the church's teachings on the subject.

Each message uses a consistent format based on the following components:

PASSAGE: Each sermon is based on a specific scripture text, which is listed for reference.

PURPOSE: Each message's central theme is summarized in one simple statement.

PREPARATION: A suggestion for a teaching tool for each object lesson is provided and, if needed, instructions are outlined.

PRESENTATION: A complete script for an interactive dialogue with children is offered.

PRAYER: A brief prayer, suitable for repetition by children, is given as a summary statement of the message.

Although the thirty sermons are listed by title in the Contents, a significant component of this collection is the section located at the back of the book which cross-references all entries by hymn stories, scripture passages, teaching tools, and theological themes.

Why is this book needed?

This book is a ready-to-use collection of messages to help children explore various aspects of the subject of death. Although books of children's sermons might include one meditation on this theme—at the most—there is no other resource that puts many explanations of the topic into one book. Since the topic of death is relevant in many ways throughout the church year, and since death occurs under many circumstances within our faith communities, this collection provides a valuable tool for the variety of occasions that demand a focus on this theme. Church leaders can readily find help for appropriate lessons, whether ideas are needed for a funeral, a memorial, a home visit, a Sunday morning talk after a significant loss, or an insightful children's story during the church year.

Who will use this book?

This book will be used in congregations by clergy, Christian educators, church school leaders, and laypersons; in parochial schools by administrators and teachers; and in homes by parents and grandparents.

Messages are designed for children in kindergarten through fifth grade but are adaptable for boys and girls in preschool and young people in the middle grades. They will also be appreciated by adults of all ages and are appropriate for intergenerational audiences.

How will this book be most helpful?

In congregations, this collection will be used as children's sermons in worship, homilies in children's church, messages in church school classes, reflections in midweek ministries, meditations in youth groups, and devotions at camp. They will also be useful as lessons in confirmation classes and Christian education programs. In parochial schools, they will be used in chapel services and classroom talks. In families, they will be helpful as a focus for mealtime devotions, faith formation, and bedtime stories.

1
Abraham's Death: Farewell to a Father

Passage: Genesis 25:7-10

Purpose: Abraham's death was a time to gather family together and celebrate their heritage.

Preparation: Family Tree

Presentation:

Have you ever completed one of these? (*Hold up an example of a "family tree" genealogical chart.*) This is a family tree. It traces the people in my family back through fathers and mothers, to grandfathers and grandmothers, as far back as I can go to find the patriarch and the matriarch of my family tree. A "patriarch" is the "first father" in a line of generations; a "matriarch" is the "first mother." In the church, we have a family tree as well. For us, as people of faith, our patriarch is Abraham. Maybe you have heard stories or sung songs about "Father Abraham."

Father Abraham lived a long life and had many descendants. That was God's promise to him, that he would be the "father of many nations." But even Father Abraham came to the time when life must end. He died and was buried in the special location he had purchased for his family's resting place. Abraham's sons, Isaac and Ishmael, gathered to say farewell to their father. Probably Abraham's relatives all shared in this time of remembering their patriarch, telling family stories, reliving memories, and thinking about the faith that Abraham taught them.

All of us have earthly fathers who will also come to a time when life ends. We are sad to say goodbye to those who have been fathers or who have been like fathers to us. When we feel sad, we can remember the story of Father Abraham. He died long ago, yet his memory still blesses people today. We have stories of our fathers to remember and to share when they are no longer on earth. We must pass along whatever was important to us about them to the generations that come after us. Most importantly, we remember that we are all connected by the power of faith that unites us in God's family tree. *(Point to family tree.)*

PRAYER:
Dear God, Thank you for the power of faith that makes our family tree strong. Help us share the memories of those we love and remind us that your love keeps us connected forever. Amen.

2
Adam and Eve's Sin: Our Redemption

Passage: Genesis 3

Purpose: Death came into the world because of sin. Eternal life comes into the world because of Jesus.

Preparation: Apple

Presentation:

Do you know what this is? (*Hold up an apple and wait for responses.*) That's right; it's an apple. In what famous story in the Bible, near the very beginning of God's Word, is an "apple" mentioned? It's in the story of Adam and Eve in the book of Genesis. Actually, the Bible just calls it a fruit, but for some reason, people have always said it was an apple. Well, God had created a perfect world and told Adam and Eve that they could eat fruit from any tree that grew there except for one. They were not supposed to eat the fruit of the knowledge of good and evil. In fact, God said that if they ate that fruit they would die.

It seems pretty simple, doesn't it? Don't eat fruit from one tree and live forever, or eat it and die. It doesn't sound like much of a choice. It would have made a lot of sense to avoid that tree, wouldn't it? (*Pause*) But what do you think they did? (*Wait for answers.*) They ate from the one tree God told them not to! They disobeyed God. And they brought sin and death into the world. Because they disobeyed God they died, and everyone after them dies, too.

That is a sad story, isn't it? But the Bible tells another story, too. It says that just as Adam and Eve brought death into the world, Jesus brings life. The Bible tells us that Jesus was perfect. He didn't disobey God. He died, but not because of his own sin; he died because of ours. And he rose from the dead so that we could have eternal life if we believe in him. The Bible says, "For as all die in Adam, so all will be made alive in Christ" (1 Corinthians 15:22). In other words, we will someday rise from the dead, just like Jesus did. Then we will live with God forever.

PRAYER:
Dear God, Thank you that the story of Adam and Eve bringing death into the world is just the beginning. We are grateful that Jesus finishes the story for us and brings us life. Amen.

3
All Saints' Day:
A Cloud of Witnesses

HYMN STORY: "For All the Saints"

PASSAGE: Hebrews 12:1

PURPOSE: All those who are faithful to God share in the joy of being called "saints."

PREPARATION: Materials to make a Picture Frame: Cardboard; Construction paper or poster board; Cotton balls; Glue; Knife or scissors; Music to "For All the Saints"; Picture to be framed; Self-adhesive picture hanger; Tape.

METHOD:

Cut a picture frame out of cardboard. To suggest the "cloud of witnesses" associated with the song, "For All the Saints," cut the frame into an oval cloud shape. Glue cotton balls to the border of one side of the frame. Tape a picture to the back side of the frame. Glue a piece of construction paper or poster board backing in place. Attach the self-adhesive picture hanger to the back of the frame.

Invite the congregation to sing the hymn before sharing the children's story.

PRESENTATION:

I want you to close your eyes. Picture inside your minds the faces of the people you know who are the most loving human beings you have ever met. Perhaps you see a member of your family, or a teacher, or someone from church. When you open your eyes, we will share the names of the people you saw. Okay, open your eyes. Whom did you see? (*Encourage the children to respond.*) You know, those people are the folks we might call "saints." And since we are celebrating "All Saints' Day," this is a good time to remember and honor the people who have helped us know what God is like, whether from our lives today or from any time in history.

(*Hold up a sample cloud frame that contains a picture of a saint from your own life.*) This person is (Name), one of God's saints. He/she is someone who has shown me what it means to be a Christian. This picture frame looks like a cloud because I want to remember the Bible lesson for All Saints' Day, that we are surrounded by a "cloud of witnesses"—saints who have come before us and who have already gone to be with God. They made the world a better place while they were here, and remembering them makes me want to help make the world a better place, too.

Many years ago, a faithful saint, a man named William Walsham How wrote words to be sung on All Saints' Day in his East London Anglican church. He tried to live a life that was a song of praise to God. And the songs that he wrote—over sixty of them—were simple and prayerful, just like his life.

Sometimes when we hear about people like Bishop How or other people we consider saints, we think that we can never be as good persons or as great saints as they were. But the truth is that all of us who say we believe and who try to follow God are called to be saints. Even if we never become famous, even if our names are not written in history books, or even if we never write beautiful hymns, we are still one with the "cloud of witnesses." Maybe that is why the tune that Ralph Vaughan Williams wrote to be sung with Bishop How's words was called *Sine Nomine*—which is Latin for "without a name." There have been so many people who have given their lives to serving God whose names we will never know, people who have passed on their faith from one generation to another, until now it has come to us.

How about you? Are you willing to become one of the saints? Then your picture can go in the cloud of witnesses, and you will help others find the joy that comes from believing in God.[1]

PRAYER:

Dear God, Thank you for all the saints who have come before us. Help us to live by faith so that we, too, can join them in praise of you. Amen.

1. Anna L. Liechty and Phyllis Vos Wezeman, adapted from "For All the Saints" in *Hymn Stories for Children: Special Days and Holidays*. (Grand Rapids, MI: Kregel Publications, 1994), 53-54.

4
Christmas's Gift: Sin's Death

Passage: Romans 6:23

Purpose: The birth of Jesus in a manger led to death for Christ on a cross and to new life for us.

Preparation: Materials to make a Chrismon: Pattern for *chi*; Pencil; Poster board, white; Scissors; Trims such as gold beads, foil, or glitter.

Method:

Trace two copies of the X-shaped *chi* pattern onto white poster board and cut out the shapes. To form the Chrismon, position one *chi* as an "X" and place the second one on top of it as a cross. Glue the two pieces together. Decorate the ornament with gold beads, foil, or glitter.

Presentation:

Have you ever made Christmas ornaments to decorate a tree? I wonder if you've ever made a special kind of ornament called a "Chrismon"? (*Hold up a sample Chrismon.*) A Chrismon uses a symbol to teach us about Jesus. This Chrismon uses the Greek letter *chi*—the first letter in the Greek word for Christ. The letter looks like an "X" to us, but in the Greek language it is called a *chi*. The "X" of the *chi* reminds us of the manger of Bethlehem. However, the second *chi* is turned so that it looks like a cross and is placed over the bottom *chi*, the X-shaped one. Together the two *chi's* create a Chrismon that reminds us of the birth of Christ in a manger at Christmas and the death of Christ on the cross before Easter. *(Trace the two symbols as they are explained.)*

It seems strange, doesn't it, to think about the death of Jesus at Christmastime? After all, when a baby is born, we think about the new life that has arrived. However, Jesus was born in order to die for us on the cross. Everyone who is born must die, but Jesus' death was different. He died so that everyone's sins could be forgiven. If Jesus hadn't given his life for us, then we wouldn't be celebrating his birth. It was the cross of Christ that gave meaning to Jesus' birth. This Chrismon reminds us of that most important truth of the Christian faith.

Of course, the greatest joy we can celebrate at Christmas is that Jesus triumphed even over death. He came to offer his life as a sacrifice for our sins and to give us a gift. When we believe in Christ, our sins are forgiven and we receive God's gift of eternal life. Like Jesus, we can triumph over death. That, indeed, is the best Christmas gift of all.

PRAYER:
Dear God, Thank you for the birth and for the death of Jesus. Help us to receive Christ's presence and to know the joy of your gift of eternal life. Amen.

5
Christ's Second Coming: A Comforting Promise

PASSAGE: John 14:1-3

PURPOSE: Jesus promises that he is preparing a place for us and will return one day to take us to be with God forever.

PREPARATION: Compass and Map

PRESENTATION:

Have you ever had to try to find your way to someplace you have never been before? Maybe you had to try to find a room at a new school or maybe a friend moved and you tried to find her new house. You could use devices like these to find your way, right? (*Hold up the compass and the map.*) A compass would be helpful to point you in the general direction of where you want to go—so long as you know whether you need to go north, south, east, or west. The map would probably be even better so that you could follow the signs and know where to turn. Would it be even better if someone who knew the way offered to go with you? (*Look for agreement.*) I think so! I would feel much better having someone show me the way and go with me on the journey.

Did you know that Jesus promised that he would come back to earth someday to show us the way to God? The idea of Jesus' return is called the "Second Coming." That simply means that Jesus will come to earth a second time—only this time not as a baby, but like a king "in clouds of glory." Jesus promised that, when he left earth, he went to prepare a place for those who believe; and someday—only God knows when—he will come to lead us safely to live in the place he has prepared for us. What a great promise!

Not only does Jesus know the way because he built the road for us to travel to God, he has walked that road himself and he will be with us when it is our time to go to God. Both a compass and a map are good tools to help us find our way, but I think a guide and a companion are even better! How wonderful that God sent us Jesus the first time; but the fact that Jesus will come back to earth a second time is an even greater gift!

PRAYER:
Dear God, Thank you for the gift of our Savior, Jesus. Thank you, too, for the promise that Jesus will come to earth again and be our guide to heaven. Amen.

6

Death's Decisions: Choosing Cremation

PASSAGE: 1 Corinthians 15:47-49

PURPOSE: Death begins a process of change for our physical bodies that cremation can hasten, while change for our spiritual bodies means being renewed in Christ.

PREPARATION: Jar of Earth

PRESENTATION:

I want to show you a miracle substance! (*Open the jar containing earth.*) Do you know what this is? (*Let the participants sniff or touch the substance.*) Yes, it is a jar of earth—a real miracle ingredient! Have you ever thought about how amazing simple dirt is? It contains the power to produce living plants, to sustain life. According to the story of creation, God brought forth Adam, the first man, from the earth. Just as the earth brings forth life, it also recycles living beings after they die. All living things decay after death and contribute to enriching the soil. We expect that cycle of life for leaves and grass, even for dead animals. When our bodies die, if we simply bury them, they, too, will return to the earth. Some people prefer to help nature's process along so that we don't use so much land for burials or spend so much money on trying to preserve the body after death. One way to speed up the body's return to the earth is called "cremation."

If someone you know has chosen to be cremated after death, there are some important things to understand. Once our spirits leave our bodies, we no longer feel pain. We are not even in our bodies after death; our spirits return to God. Our bodies are like a favorite suit of clothing that we have outgrown. We just can't use them anymore. If, after death, a body is cremated, that means what is left behind is simply placed in a special fire that is very hot. Since our bodies are 90 percent water, the shell that is left mostly evaporates. What is left behind is simply ashes. When people choose to be cremated, their families receive a container from the crematory that contains their cremains, or their remaining ashes. Those ashes may be kept in a special urn by the family, buried in a small plot of ground, or spread in a favorite place to return to the earth.

Cremation is not what everyone chooses, but some people think it makes sense. The Christian, as well as the Hebrew Scriptures, teach us that our physical bodies are made from dust and must return to the earth. Our spiritual bodies, however, are eternal and are given new life in Christ—meaning it isn't important what happens with our earthly bodies. The body that will live forever in heaven is the spiritual one. We will change where we live, that's all. Therefore, what we decide to do with our old worn-out suit of clothes doesn't matter. It was made from things of the earth and it will return to the earth. The process for the body to be recycled is part of God's plan. But don't worry: God has an even better plan for our transformation in heaven.

PRAYER:
Dear God, Thank you for the miracle of earth's cycle of life. Help us to completely trust you for the life we will be given in heaven. Amen.

7
Easter's Promise: Eternal Life

PASSAGE: Matthew 28:1-7; Mark 16:1-8; Luke 24:1-12; John 20:1-10

PURPOSE: Christ's resurrection gives us the promise of eternal life.

PREPARATION: Easter Lily Bulb; Easter Lily

PRESENTATION:

Does this look like a promise to you? *(Hold up the flower bulb.)* This is a flower bulb—an Easter lily bulb, to be exact. Can you guess what happens to this bulb if you plant it in the ground? Yes, it turns into a beautiful flower, like this! *(Display an Easter lily.)* These are the flowers we think of first when we think of Easter. In fact, they are called "Easter lilies" because they bloom in the spring and they are used to decorate our churches and our homes at Easter time.

The message of Jesus' resurrection is symbolized for us in the Easter lily. When planted in the ground, the bulb dies, but from it comes a new bulb and eventually a new flower. This reminds us that even though Jesus died, he rose to new life on Easter Sunday. The pure white color of the lily symbolizes the new hope we have to be forgiven, to be washed clean of our sins, and to rise to new life with Jesus. Even the shape of the lily reminds us of the Easter story—the flower looks like a trumpet, announcing the Good News that Jesus is raised from the dead!

Although on Good Friday we mourn the death of Jesus, on Easter Sunday we celebrate that Jesus gained the victory over death. We no longer have to fear death because Jesus promises that if we believe in him we, too, will receive eternal life. Christians know that death is not the end, but only a new beginning—just like planting this bulb is not the end of its life, but a glorious new beginning of something beautiful. Now, when we see the Easter lily, we can remember that it represents new life in Christ, a reminder that death is nothing to be feared. Jesus is triumphant over death, and because he lives, we will live with God—forever!

PRAYER:
Dear God, Thank you for the symbols of new life all around us. Help us to remember Jesus' promise that we will live with him forever. Amen.

8
Empty Chair: A Classmate's Death

PASSAGE: Job 1:21b

PURPOSE: Accepting the reality of death frees us to embrace the importance of God's gift of life.

PREPARATION: Chair

PRESENTATION:

Do you have an assigned seat at church or school? *(Point to a chair.)* Sometimes teachers can take attendance just by looking to see which chairs are empty as class begins. Having a seat that is our own marks our place in a group. That is a good thing. However, when someone dies the empty chair can symbolize our loss and the empty place in our lives. It seems so wrong when a young person, who is still in school and still learning about life, dies. Our classmate's empty chair can be a very difficult reminder that no one lives forever and even young people can die.

Maybe you have seen movies or television programs that include a funeral service or a burial scene. Often the script will contain a phrase from the book of Job in the Hebrew Scriptures: "The Lord gave, and the Lord has taken away; blessed be the name of the Lord." Without someone to explain those words, listeners may come to the conclusion that death is somehow God's fault, yet we're supposed to love God despite our feelings of loss and sadness. The point of the scripture is that life is God's gift and no one knows just how long our lives on earth will last. When we come to understand that each person is on earth for a limited amount of time, then we can really begin to value the lives of all of those around us—classmates, family, friends, and neighbors.

However, the point to remember is that God gives us life on earth to cherish for a brief time; then God grants us the gift of eternal life. We must remember to trust God with things we cannot understand —like the death of someone who seems too young to die. Even more importantly, we must remember to treasure life each day because we know it doesn't last forever. Life is God's gift; our life and the lives of those around us are the blessings God gives us to value for a time. We must treasure those who fill the chairs as well as remember those who once filled the chairs that are now empty.

PRAYER:
Dear God, Thank you for the lives of each of our family and friends. Help us to remember that life is your gift to us each day. Amen.

9
Epiphany's Message: Jesus' Mission

PASSAGE: 1 Corinthians 15:26

PURPOSE: Each treasure that the Wise Men presented to Jesus reveals that Christ came to be our King, High Priest, and Savior.

PREPARATION: Gifts—Gold, Frankincense, and Myrrh

Gold could be represented by metal slugs or spray-painted stones set in a box. Incense, even frankincense-scented, can be placed in a decorative container. Myrrh might be depicted by scented oil in a jar or perfumed liquid in a fancy bottle.

PRESENTATION:

Why do you think I have three gifts today? (*Display the three gifts.*) We're celebrating a special festival in the church called Epiphany, the day we remember an event that occurred in the life of Jesus. Who visited Jesus and his mother and father and brought him gifts? (*Encourage someone to answer the Magi or Three Kings or Wise Men.*) Do you know what gifts they brought to Jesus? (*Allow the children to answer: gold, frankincense, and myrrh.*)

Here is one of the gifts they brought. What is it supposed to represent? (*Hold up the gold.*) You know, gold is a gift fit for a king, isn't it? The Wise Men knew that Jesus was destined to be a king because they had seen the signs in the heavens. What sign did they see that led them to Jesus? *(The star.)* Gold is an easy gift to understand. Let's look at the next one. *(Hold up the incense. Allow the children to smell and touch it, even to light some in a safe container under careful supervision.)* Do you know what it is? With the gift of frankincense, the Wise Men recognized that Jesus was to be a religious leader. Incense was used in worship in the temple. It was burned by the high priest to make an offering to God. As Christians we say that Jesus is our "High Priest." The Wise Men gave him a gift that was just right, didn't they? The last gift could have been the most expensive one of all. *(Hold up the myrrh.)* Does anyone know what the third gift is called? *(Myrrh.)* Myrrh is very expensive oil used to prepare a body for burial. It seems a little strange to us, and sad, because it's not the way we do things today. But in Jesus' day, this would have been a very special treasure to be saved all your life. In a way, the Wise Men seemed to be saying that they understood that Jesus was born to die to become our Savior.

Let's name the three gifts again. *(Hold up each gift as it is highlighted.)* Gold—a gift for a king; Frankincense—a gift for a priest; Myrrh—a precious gift for our Savior. These three gifts help us understand even more about who Jesus was born to be. They "awaken" or "reveal" to us who Jesus is—our king, our high priest, and our savior! And that's what "Epiphany" means—an "awakening" or "revelation." Now you can be even wiser than you were before because you understand the value of knowing Jesus![1]

PRAYER:
Dear God, Thank you for the special meaning that Jesus' life brings to our lives. Amen.

1. Judith Harris Chase, Anna L. Liechty, and Phyllis Vos Wezeman, adapted from "Treasure Chest" in *Festival of Faith: A Vacation Church School Curriculum Celebrating the Gifts of God.* (Prescott, AZ: Educational Ministries, Inc., 1993), 103-105.

10
Faithful Hands:
A Grandparent's Death

HYMN STORY: "Precious Lord, Take My Hand"

PASSAGE: Isaiah 41:13

PURPOSE: We can face life's unknown path when we trust God's faithful hand to guide us on our journey.

PREPARATION: Used Work Glove
Music to "Precious Lord, Take My Hand"
   Invite the congregation to sing the hymn before sharing the children's story.

PRESENTATION:

Can you tell anything about the person who owned this glove? (*Allow the participants to speculate about the size of the person's hand or the type of work he or she might have done.*) Even though this glove seems to hold the shape of the hand of the person who used it, we really can't tell too much about the kind of person he or she might have been. We could tell much more if we could see the hands of the person, couldn't we? Hands can be large or small, rough or smooth, gentle or hardworking, young or old. Hands are a very important means of communication between human beings. We appreciate the touch of love and care we receive from our family members. It is comforting to hold our parent's or grandparent's hand when we are afraid of the dark or when we're crossing a busy street. When we lose a grandparent in death, however, we may desperately miss the hand that guided us, the hand we held on to when we needed to feel safe or special.

One way to find help when a grandparent dies is to think about the fact that the one we love is now in God's hands. Just as we took our grandparents' hands once to cross the street, we can imagine our grandmother or grandfather reaching out to be led by God to a new existence in heaven. One song often sung in our grandparents' churches is still enjoyed today. The title is "Precious Lord, Take My Hand." Thomas Dorsey, or "Georgia Tom" as he was known by his fellow jazz musicians, wrote the song soon after he experienced the tragic death of his young wife and infant son. In his grief, Thomas Dorsey sat at the piano playing a familiar tune and repeating the phrase "Blessed Lord," simply looking for comfort. His friend suggested that he try the word "precious" instead of "blessed." Soon the lines to the song formed in his mind, and he wrote the most famous song of his 250 gospel hymns.

Dorsey's song became an immediate success after people at the Pilgrim Baptist Church in Chicago heard his new song the following week. All of us need the reassurance that we have a hand to hold when we face difficult times in life. On earth, clasping hands with our grandparents can provide a sense of security and peace. When the time comes that we must say goodbye, we need to remember that God reaches out to them and to us. God can lead us through the storms of life and, when it's time, God can lead us home.

PRAYER:
Dear God, Thank you for creating hands to hold. Help us to understand that you also hold us in your hands. Amen.

11
Funeral Service: Final Farewell

PASSAGE: Revelation 14:13

PURPOSE: Funeral rituals help us to accept the finality of death and to express the reality of faith.

PREPARATION: Memorial Card

PRESENTATION:

Do you know what happens at a funeral? (*Let the listeners share ideas.*) When someone dies, it is a sad time for the families and friends. Funerals are the way we try to help each other say goodbye and find comfort in our sorrow. Because people are different, funerals can be different, too. Often relatives plan funerals, but sometimes people plan their own services before they die. They may want specific music or special readings. They may want the body present or not, the casket open so that the body can be viewed, or not. They may want to wear certain clothes or be buried with favorite possessions. Sometimes the service is held in a church; sometimes the service occurs in the funeral parlor or at another special location. The important thing is that family and friends have a way to celebrate the memory of the person who has passed away. Funerals also help us understand that the person's death is real and that we must say goodbye one final time.

Although each celebration is different, there are many experiences common to most funerals. Before a funeral, there is usually something called a "wake," a time for people to gather to visit with relatives and perhaps view the body that once held the spirit of their family member or friend. That's why we also call this time the "viewing" or "visitation." At a wake, you may see one of these. (*Hold up the memorial card.*) This is a memorial card. It contains information about the person who has died, like when he or she was born and the date of death. There may be a favorite scripture or poem to read, or even a picture as a remembrance. At the wake, you may see photographs displayed that were taken throughout a person's life, and you may see special objects that represent their hobbies or interests. The point of this time of visitation is that we get an opportunity to focus on what was important to the person as a way to honor the memory we share.

At a funeral, as we share loving memories, we affirm our faith. The Spirit promises that those who live for God will be blessed in heaven. That is truly something to celebrate!

PRAYER:
Dear God, Help us in the sad times of funerals to know the joy that comes from celebrating the hope of eternal life. Amen.

12
God's Faithfulness: Anniversary Memories

PASSAGE: Joshua 4:4-7

PURPOSE: On the anniversary of the death of a loved one, memories offer an opportunity to recall God's faithfulness.

PREPARATION: Children's Book – *Wilfrid Gordon McDonald Partridge* by Mem Fox and Julie Vivas, Illustrator. Kane/Miller Book Publishers, 1985.

PRESENTATION:
Have you ever read the book *Wilfrid Gordon McDonald Partridge?* (*Display the book and show the pictures while telling the story.*) It's the story of a young boy who lives next door to a senior citizens' home. Although he makes friends with all of his neighbors, his favorite resident is "Miss Nancy" because she has four names, too—Nancy Allison Delacourt Cooper. One day Wilfrid overheard his father and mother talking about Miss Nancy. "Poor old thing," they said. "She's lost her memory." When Wilfrid asked his family and friends, "What's a memory?" he received many answers. It's something from long ago that makes you laugh; makes you cry; makes you feel warm; and something that's precious as gold. Wilfrid searched through his house for special items, placed them in a basket, and brought them to Miss Nancy. One by one, she took each object in her hands and remembered important events in her life that brought warm feelings to her heart and special memories to her mind.

One of the ways to face the anniversary of the death of a loved one is to recall memories about the special person on that important day. It might help to look at pictures or scrapbooks from "long ago." It could involve visiting with family and friends and "laughing" about happy times with a grandfather or grandmother. It may include a visit to the cemetery to place flowers on the grave of a friend, which might make us "cry." We can feel "warm" as we hold a handmade gift, like a drawing from a brother or sister. And time spent sorting through a collection a parent enjoyed could be "precious as gold."

Anniversaries are a good time to remember someone who has died and memories are a wonderful way to insure that the special person is never forgotten. Whether it's been one year, or two, or many more since the death of a loved one, it is especially important to use the time to remember the faithfulness of God—every day of our lives.

PRAYER:
Dear God, Thank you for the memories of our loved ones that we recall in our heads, hold in our hands, and treasure in our hearts. Amen.

13
God's Shelter: Facing a Disaster

PASSAGE: Isaiah 43:2-3a

PURPOSE: Despite the disasters that can happen in the world, we must remember that God is always with us.

PREPARATION: Disaster Kit (Include supplies such as gas mask, rubber gloves, and surgical mask)

PRESENTATION:

I've gathered all sorts of safety supplies because we never know when disaster may strike. (*Open the kit and begin putting on the various pieces of disaster equipment.*) Who knows, we could have an earthquake, a fire, a flood, or a tornado. We could even be the targets for a terrorist! (*Put on a ridiculous amount of "precautions."*) Now I'm prepared in case of an emergency. Life is very dangerous, you know! What do you think? Is it reasonable for me to live like this? Could I eat and sleep and live my life wearing these? (*Give respondents an opportunity to react.*)

The truth is that life is very dangerous. There have always been disasters and tragedies as long as people have been on the earth. Just because we are God's people doesn't mean we will never experience the difficulties that life in this world can bring. People get hurt; people lose their homes, their possessions, or even their lives. However, we can not live our lives in fear of what might happen! In fact, the prophet Isaiah reminds us in the Hebrew Scriptures that God promises to go through the flood or the fire with us. We do not have to live in fear because, whatever happens, we are not alone.

That doesn't mean that it is wrong to plan ahead or to be prepared for an emergency. God counts on us to use the good minds we have been given and to use our common sense. However, people of faith recognize that not all of life's emergencies can be prevented or controlled. The challenge is not to let our fears control us. Instead, we place our trust in the One who is in total control of life—whether we are with God on earth or with God in the life to come.

PRAYER:

Dear God, Help us when we are afraid because of bad things that happen. Remind us that we are never alone—that you are always with us. Amen.

14
Good Friday's Gift: Forgiveness

PASSAGE: Matthew 27:45-46; Mark 15:33-41; Luke 23:44-49; John 19:28-37

PURPOSE: Jesus accepted death on a cross in order to provide the gift of forgiveness.

PREPARATION: Nails

PRESENTATION:

I have a gift for everyone today! (*Hold up a handful of nails.*) Actually, the nail is just a reminder of the gift we each receive on Good Friday. You know, don't you, that Jesus was nailed to a cross on Good Friday. It is hard to think about Jesus dying. The story of his death makes us sad. We don't understand sometimes why Jesus had to die, and if he was God's son, why did God let that happen? The hard truth is that God is just and that sin must be punished. All human beings sin, including you and me. But Good Friday means that if we accept Jesus as our Savior, then his death on the cross covers our debt of sin. Jesus was crucified so that we could receive forgiveness for our sin.

It wasn't the nails that held Jesus to the cross. Jesus was God's son. He could have asked God for all of heaven's angels to come and rescue him but he did not. Jesus accepted death on the cross because he loves us. It was love that held Jesus on the cross—love for you and for me.

It seems strange to call the day that Jesus died "Good" Friday, but it is good for us that Jesus was willing to die to pay the price for sin. With our nails we can create a simple cross. (*Use two nails to form a cross.*) The cross becomes a reminder of Jesus' gift—the gift of his life. And it also reminds us of Jesus' love. He loved us so much that he was willing to lay down his life so that we might be sure of God's forgiveness. The cross reminds us that our sins are paid in full by Jesus. That's an amazing gift of love!

PRAYER:
Dear God, Thank you for Good Friday's reminder of Jesus' love. We accept his gift of forgiveness. Amen.

15
Heavenly Bodies: Our Transfiguration

PASSAGE: Matthew 27:1-13

PURPOSE: Like the disciples' experience on the Mount of Transfiguration, heaven will be a place where we are known to God and to one another.

PREPARATION: Baby Picture

PRESENTATION:

Do you recognize the face in this picture? (*Show the baby picture and allow the participants to respond.*) Would you know if I gave you a hint? You're sitting very near this person, but s/he may not look exactly like this anymore. Give up? It's me! This is my baby picture! Do you see the resemblance now? I have changed a good bit on the outside, but I am the same person on the inside.

Jesus' disciples once experienced an amazing change in their leader. In the Bible the story is called "The Transfiguration." "Transfigure" means "to change in appearance." Jesus had climbed to the top of a mountain for some time alone with God. He took Peter, James, and John with him. While Jesus was on the mountain something amazing happened. He changed right before the disciples' eyes: his clothes turned to dazzling white. Suddenly, the disciples saw Moses and Elijah standing with Jesus. How do you suppose they knew what Moses and Elijah looked like? We really don't know the answer to that question, do we?

Maybe their experience helps us understand what heaven will be like. Our physical bodies will be changed to spiritual bodies, and at this point we can only imagine what they might be like. But perhaps others will simply "know" who we are, like Peter and the others simply "knew" who the two people standing with Jesus were. Or perhaps others will recognize something in our being that is familiar, like we might recognize someone from a baby picture. The point is that in heaven we will be different: changed, like Jesus was on the Mount of Transfiguration. And we will somehow be able to know one another just as God knows each one of us. The important message from the lesson, however, is that Jesus is the one who knows the way to God. We are to listen to him. If we listen and follow, we will find the way to heaven and our own transfiguration.

PRAYER:
Dear God, Thank you for sending Jesus to prepare us for heaven. Help us to listen to Jesus and to follow him each day. Amen.

16
Jesus' Burial: Joseph's Compassion

PASSAGE: Matthew 27:57-60; Mark 15:42-46; Luke 23:50-53; John 19:38-42

PURPOSE: Like Joseph of Arimathea cared for Jesus' body after death, funeral directors today care for the earthly remains of those who have died.

PREPARATION: Bible
Yellow Pages Phone Book

PRESENTATION:

Let's open our Bible to the New Testament and read a few verses from each of the Gospels. We'll start with Matthew 27:57-60, continue with Mark 15:42-46, then Luke 23:50-53, and conclude with John 19:38-42. (*Look up each passage and read the texts.*) What did we learn about Joseph, the caretaker of Jesus' body after the crucifixion? Matthew and Luke tell us that he was from the Jewish town of Arimathea. They add that he was a rich man who was a good and righteous person. These two Gospels reveal that Joseph was a respected member of the Council, and Luke adds the important line that he had not agreed to their plan with respect to Jesus' death. Matthew and Luke also report that Joseph was waiting expectantly for the Kingdom of God. Mark and John share that Joseph was a disciple of Jesus, but a secret one because of his fear of the Jews.

All four books indicate that Joseph went to Pilate and asked, boldly, for the body of Jesus to prepare it for burial. He took the body, wrapped it in a clean linen cloth, laid it in his own new tomb hewn in the rock—where no one had ever laid—and rolled a great stone in front of the opening. John indicates that Nicodemus, a fellow follower, came with a mixture of myrrh and aloes—approximately one hundred pounds—and helped Joseph prepare Jesus' body for burial.

In our day, a person like Joseph—one who cares for the body of someone who has died—is called a funeral director. Sometimes this person is also called an embalmer, mortician, or undertaker. If we look in the yellow pages of the phone book, we can find a list of the funeral directors in our area. *(Show pages in phone book.)* A funeral director prepares human bodies for burial or cremation and organizes all of the arrangements during this process. He or she works with the family to plan the service and to select the casket, vault, and cemetery plot. This person obtains the death certificate and burial permit and prepares the obituary notice, register book, and memorial folders. The funeral director arranges flowers, cares for the family, greets mourners, instructs pallbearers, arranges transportation, and much more.

As we read the accounts of the life of Jesus' caretaker, Joseph of Arimathea, and remember the important work of funeral directors today, let us thank God for people who share their convictions through their compassion.

PRAYER:
Dear God, Thank you for people who care for us during the difficult times of life. Amen.

17
Jesus' Stories: A Lost Pet

PASSAGE: Luke 15:3-7

PURPOSE: Jesus used stories about animals to assure us of a loving God who cares for all creation.

PREPARATION: Shepherd's Crook

PRESENTATION:

No one likes to lose anything, right? This tool helps a shepherd keep the sheep from getting lost. *(If possible, hold up a shepherd's crook or show a picture of one.)* A shepherd's crook helps a shepherd bring lambs back to the flock if they start to wander away. Jesus once told a story of a shepherd who left the ninety-nine sheep in the fold in order to look for just one that was missing. Jesus' story teaches us that—like the lost lamb—each person is important to God. Jesus is the Good Shepherd who came in order to find those people who were lost and to bring them safely to God.

We are comforted to know that God loves each person so much. But we can also be comforted in another way by Jesus' story. A loving God cares about all creation. That means God cares about animals, too. When we lose a pet through death, we can know that God cares about our loss—and about our pet. Nothing we do can bring our pet back. Of course we will be sad. We may cry or feel angry or lonely. But God understands our feelings. And God gives us loving people in our lives who can help us think and talk about our loss.

We won't ever forget a pet that we have loved. We will have stories to share, maybe even pictures to place in a scrapbook, or special objects like a collar or a toy to keep as a treasured memory. If we remember that Jesus understood our love for animals, then we can be assured that God cares for our pets in ways that we may not know or understand right now. But we can trust God to care for all of God's creation—including you and me.

PRAYER:
Dear God, Help us to know that you care for each one of your creations. Comfort us when we feel the loss of animals we love. Amen.

18
Lazarus's Death: Grieving a Sibling

PASSAGE: John 11:21

PURPOSE: Even though we have the hope of eternal life, the death of someone close to us brings grief that we must endure.

PREPARATION: Materials to make Footsteps: Construction paper; Markers; Pencil; Scissors.

METHOD:
Cut five pieces of construction paper into footprint shapes. Although they may be any color, they should be the same size. Write one of the following words on each footprint: Denial, Anger, Bargaining, Depression, Acceptance.

PRESENTATION:
Have you ever tried learning to dance by following the footsteps? *(Hold up the footstep patterns with the blank side showing; even try a dance step, if possible.)* It isn't easy to learn the steps from a diagram, but by following the directions and listening to the music, we can sometimes figure it out. It's easier if we have someone to help guide us through the dance steps, isn't it? Dance steps follow a pattern, just as many of life's experiences do, both happy ones and sad ones. There is even a pattern to the experience people have after the death of some-

one close to them. A woman by the name of Dr. Elisabeth Kubler-Ross studied the process that people go through in dealing with grief, the sad feelings we must cope with when someone we love—like a brother or a sister—has died.

Dr. Kubler-Ross discovered that there are five stages or steps to the grief process that human beings must cope with as they work through their grief. *(Hold up the footprint as each stage is discussed.)* Often people begin with "Denial"—that is when we say "This can't be happening!" and we hope we will wake up to discover it was all a bad dream. Another step we take in dealing with grief is "Anger"—that is when we get mad at the person who has died for leaving us, or mad at other people, maybe even God. "Bargaining" is a step we might take when we know someone is going to die—that means we try to make a deal with God to keep our loved one alive, like "I'll always eat my vegetables and I'll never miss Sunday school." Yet another step in the process is "Depression"—when we turn our anger inside and really become sad, so sad we can barely move or think or even eat or sleep. All of these stages can occur in any order, and like a dance we sometimes repeat a step that we have been through before. The last remaining step of grief is "Acceptance"—when we come to understand that death is real and something that we must face the best we can. Understanding that these steps represent normal ways that human beings come to terms with death and dying can help us be more gentle with ourselves and others as we deal with the loss of someone close to us, even someone as close as a brother or a sister.

Although Dr. Kubler-Ross wrote about the stages of grief in the 1960s, the Christian Scriptures show us that long ago Jesus understood the grief we feel. When Mary and Martha's brother Lazarus died, they were upset—even angry and depressed—over the loss of their sibling. John, one of the Gospel writers, tells the story of how deeply Jesus sympathized with the grief they were experiencing, saying "Jesus wept" with them. Although Jesus raised Lazarus from the dead and restored Mary and Martha's brother for a time, at a later point Lazarus would have died. Even though the sisters had a deep faith in Jesus' power to take care of their brother in heaven, Mary and Martha probably felt sad all over again. Grief is simply something we must go through when someone we love has died. The difference for Christians is that we have Jesus to guide us through the steps as we deal with the reality of our loss. Like a dance, the steps are easier to follow when we have a partner.

PRAYER:

Dear God, Thank you that Jesus understands our grief. Help us to follow his lead as we learn to express our feelings of loss when someone we love has died. Amen.

19
Memorial Day: Honoring Heroes

PASSAGE: Romans 13:7a, c

PURPOSE: To preserve the ideals we cherish, God asks us to honor those worthy of respect; our country asks us to remember those who have sacrificed their lives for the cause of freedom.

PREPARATION: Memorial Wreath

PRESENTATION:

Have you ever seen a wreath like this? *(Hold up memorial wreath.)* It isn't a Christmas wreath, is it? Do you know where a wreath like this might be used? *(If necessary, hint that they may have seen this type of wreath at a floral shop or in a cemetery.)* This kind of wreath is used to honor those who have died, especially the men and women who sacrificed their lives in service to their country. On Memorial Day, people in the United States pay tribute to these individuals. If you visit a cemetery on Memorial Day, you will see many gravesites that have been freshly cleaned up and that have flowers or wreaths placed in memory of the person buried there. This is a custom or tradition that had its beginnings in our nation's history. After the Civil War people began decorating the graves of soldiers who died. The first "Decoration Day," as it was called then, was May 30, 1868. Through the years the name has changed to Memorial Day and instead of May 30, it is now observed on the last Monday in May. The purpose, however, is the same: to honor our country's dead, especially those who have given their lives in the cause of preserving freedom.

So Memorial Day is not a religious holiday; and yet we cannot think about the nation's heroes or our loved ones who have died, without also thinking about God. The Christian Scriptures teach us that God wants us to honor those who have earned respect. Perhaps God knows that by remembering the good and noble principles our heroes and leaders have stood for, we can continue to live with more honor ourselves.

As Christians, we pray for peace and seek to avoid war. However, we understand that sometimes the very peace we enjoy has come because someone else was willing to stand in defense of our country. So we lay wreaths on soldiers' and loved ones' graves—not because they are in those graves and see our efforts—but because we become better people ourselves in the act of remembering and respecting them. If the freedom and honor they stood for is to continue, then we must be the ones to carry those ideals into our daily battles.

PRAYER:
Dear God, Thank you for the brave lives of those who have come before us. Help us, as well, to live in service to others. Amen.

20
Nature's Lesson: New Beginnings

HYMN STORY: "Hymn of Promise"

PASSAGE: Ecclesiastes 3:1-8

PURPOSE: Nature teaches the spiritual truth that in every end there is a beginning.

PREPARATION: Materials to make Two-part Puzzles: Cardboard, cereal or shirt boxes, or 5" x 7" index cards; Crayons or markers; Manila envelope; Music for "Hymn of Promise"; Scissors.

METHOD:

Make and use simple two-part puzzles as the teaching tools for the children's sermon that highlights the song, "Hymn of Promise."

Cut cardboard into five-inch by seven-inch pieces, or use five-inch by seven-inch index cards for the project. Once the pieces are cut, draw a wiggly line down the center of each rectangle. Illustrate some of the ideas from the hymn text on the puzzle pieces. For example, on the left side of one puzzle, draw a bulb, and on the right side depict a flower. Be sure to include the following combinations as well: seed and apple tree; cocoon and butterfly; cross and empty tomb.

Last, cut each rectangle apart along the wiggly line to create a two-piece puzzle. Mix up the pieces and try putting them together by matching each pair's "end" and its "beginning." Store the puzzle pieces in a manila envelope.

Invite the congregation to sing the hymn before sharing the children's story.

Presentation:

I have a game for us to play. Perhaps you can help me complete this puzzle. The idea is to match the two symbols that go together. We might be able to tell by just looking at the symbol, but each puzzle piece will only fit with the one that is the correct answer. Let's look at each piece and see if we can figure it out. (*Hold up each piece and name the symbol. Then choose enough participants to help match the correct pieces.*)

Can you find the one that matches the flower? How do you know the bulb matches the flower? (*Let the puzzle player answer, "Because flowers come from bulbs."*) What about the apple? Why does the seed match? (*Let someone answer, "Because apple trees grow from seeds."*) Then we know what goes with the butterfly, but why would these two be partners? (*Let a participant answer, "Because butterflies come from cocoons."*) You are all really smart!

Really, all of these symbols teach us the same lesson. Can you guess what it is? (*Listen to speculations.*) Actually, I was thinking that these symbols from nature teach us that the end is just the beginning. When a plant dies in the fall, all that is left is the dead looking bulb. Yet in the spring, that dead looking bulb becomes a flower! On the other hand, when an apple falls to the ground, the outer layer rots away leaving only the seeds. Yet in time, those seeds can produce new apple trees that blossom and produce more fruit! And we all know that the caterpillar seems to die inside a cocoon, but soon the caterpillar becomes a new creature transformed into a beautiful butterfly! What seems to be the end, each time becomes a new beginning! Nature teaches us that life only seems temporary. Life does come to an end for all living things; death is a natural part of the process of life. However, death is not the last word. The powerful creative force of nature brings new life from what only seems dead. This lesson we observe in nature prepares us to understand the message God shared through the life and death of Jesus.

(*Hold up the additional puzzle pieces containing the cross and the tomb.*) Can you explain why these two symbols are related? (*Wait while participants explain the story of Jesus' death and resurrection. Let one begin and another add to the story, filling in details as needed.*) Exactly! As Jesus died on the cross, what looked like the end of Jesus' life was actually a new beginning for everyone. Jesus rose from the dead and promised that those who believe will have eternal life, too.

All of these symbols are found in a song called "Hymn of Promise." Natalie Sleeth wrote this hymn after she had been thinking a lot about the message of hope found in nature. She looked at flowers and fruit and butterflies. She read poetry and talked about the mysteries of life with friends. The result was the poetry set to music that she called "Hymn of Promise."

Sometimes we don't know how God will solve the puzzle of life's mysteries. But whenever we feel that we have reached an end, we should look at flowers, apples, and butterflies, and remember that in each end is a beginning—just as the empty tomb teaches us to remember that even death is simply the beginning of eternal life. That is God's promise to each of us.[1]

PRAYER:
Dear God, Thank you for the message in nature that life continues. Thank you for the message of Jesus that eternal life is ours. Amen.

1. Anna L. Liechty and Phyllis Vos Wezeman, adapted from "Hymn of Promise," *Hymn Stories for Children: Lent and Easter.* (Pittsburgh, PA: LOGOS System Associates, Inc., 2002), 37-38.

21
Paul's Prophecy: Facing Life's Questions

PASSAGE: 1 Corinthians 13:12

PURPOSE: Paul promises that one day we will see God face to face and understand life more clearly.

PREPARATION: Mirror

PRESENTATION:

Do you look in a mirror every day? I know I do. (*Hold up a mirror.*) Do you ever wonder how other people say you've changed when the face in the mirror each day looks exactly the same as the one you saw yesterday? We usually can't see our own changes because we grow and change in such small ways moment by moment. Sometimes we notice the changes in other people, however—especially the changes we see happening in the lives of those who are sick or suffering. Then we wish we could go back in time to see them again the way they were before they lost weight or lost hair, before they looked so sick. The truth is, though, that we are all changing all the time. We just don't usually notice the changes that much.

When someone we know and love is changing because the person is struggling with an illness, even facing death, watching him or her change can be very difficult. We wonder why the person we love has to suffer. We don't understand why prayers don't seem to help or why the person we pray for doesn't seem to be getting any better. Saint Paul wrote in Corinthians that trying to understand life's mysteries is like looking in a dark mirror, one that doesn't reflect light very well anymore. *(If possible, produce a mirror with damaged silvering.)* Paul suggests that on earth we won't be able to see God's face—meaning we won't understand God's plan or purpose clearly. But Paul promises that someday—in heaven—we will know God's will perfectly, just like God already understands our questions and concerns.

No matter how our faces change over time, we are still the same people on the inside. This is true of the people we know who are changing more rapidly because they are battling illness or disease. They are still the same people on the inside. And who they are on the inside is the part that never changes, the part of them that we love, the part of them that is eternal and will get to see God face-to-face in heaven.

PRAYER:
Dear God, We understand that change is part of life. Help us to trust your love to be with us through all the changes we must face. Amen.

22
Pentecost's Power: The Holy Spirit's Comfort

PASSAGE: John 14:16

PURPOSE: Jesus sends the Holy Spirit to be with us in all of life's experiences.

PREPARATION: Comforter

PRESENTATION:

Do you have a favorite comforter that you use to help you feel better? *(Hold up the comforter.)* Maybe it's your favorite blanket from when you were little? All of us need comforting now and then, especially when someone we love dies. At Pentecost, the disciples were having a hard time because Jesus had been crucified. They knew he had been raised from the dead, but he told them he had to leave. So on Pentecost they were gathered together in an Upper Room, not really knowing what to do. Probably they were feeling somewhat sad and confused.

But Jesus had promised them that he would not leave them all alone like orphans, comfortless. He said he would send a helper to be with them always—God's Holy Spirit. Another word to describe the Holy Spirit is "Comforter"—someone who comes to our aid, to encourage us and to assure us that we can keep going. This is what the Holy Spirit did for the disciples at Pentecost. They were filled with enthusiasm and new hope so that they could leave their Upper Room and proclaim the Good News that Jesus was alive.

The Holy Spirit is still with us today. And when we turn to Christ for help, we receive the promised Holy Spirit—our Comforter—who will encourage and assure us through our difficult times. Like the disciples in the Upper Room, we must pray and open our hearts to welcome God's Spirit. Then like a favorite blanket, God's love enfolds us and helps us to find the comfort we need to face life's challenges.

PRAYER:

Dear God, Thank you for the promise of your Holy Spirit. Help us to open our lives to receive the Spirit's comforting presence. Amen.

23
Preparation for Burial: Finding Comfort

PASSAGE: Luke 23:55-24:1

PURPOSE: From the moment of death to the closing of the grave, those who grieve can find comfort in the traditions of preparing a loved one's body for burial.

PREPARATION: Travel Kit

PRESENTATION:
When you go on a trip, do you or the people in your family ever pack one of these? *(Hold up the travel kit.)* You've seen a travel kit before, right? Why do we need to take along these items? *(Allow the participants to speculate about the use of some of the items.)* Yes, our bodies require constant care, don't they? This is true all our lives, and it is even true when we die.

Maybe you have had someone in your family, or a friend, die and you wondered what happened to the body after death. Just like we prepare our bodies in everyday life, the body must be prepared for burial. Today, people contact a person called a funeral director who will come and pick up the body and do the special cleansing and preparation required. Families must choose the coffin, or container for the body. People usually want flowers and a special service to remember the life of the person who died. Music, pictures, pallbearers—friends or relatives to carry the coffin to the final resting place—even the cemetery plot and a headstone or marker are all decisions that someone must make. Even though this is a lot to think about, preparing a loved one's body for burial can be helpful to those who are grieving. Arranging details for the burial of the one we have lost in death allows us to say goodbye to the earthly remains.

All of Jesus' followers were very sad when Jesus died on the cross— as we all are when someone we love dies. The women who traveled with Jesus and the disciples went to Jesus' tomb to prepare his body with spices, which was the way they cleansed their dead and readied them for burial in those times. Of course, when they arrived at the tomb, they discovered that Jesus had risen—his body was not there. That is the message we take with us to the cemetery as we carry the body of our loved one to its final resting place. Often pastors lead the grieving family and friends in a graveside service, committing the body to the earth and the person's soul to God. We know that death is only a journey to a new and better place because Jesus triumphed over death.

PRAYER:
Dear God, Thank you for those who help families during their time of grief. Remind us that Jesus triumphed over death so that we may have the hope of eternal life. Amen.

24
Psalm Twenty-Three: Words of Comfort

PASSAGE: Psalm 23

PURPOSE: When grief washes over us anew, we can find comfort in God's abiding presence.

PREPARATION: Conch Shell

PRESENTATION:

Do you know that you can hear the sound of the ocean in a conch shell? (*Hold shell to ear and listen.*) Listen yourselves and you will hear the ocean, too. (*Allow others to try.*) It seems like magic, and yet there is a simple explanation. What sounds like waves at the ocean are really the noises from inside your own body echoing in the chambers of the shell. The sound "triggers" our memory of ocean waves washing against the shore, so we think that is what we hear. The idea of ocean waves can teach us something about grief, as well.

When someone dies we often compare the depth of our sadness to the depth of the ocean. We may search for and find comfort in many places—maybe the stanza of a hymn, a line from a prayer, or words of scripture. One of the most familiar passages from the Bible, often read at a funeral, comes from Psalm Twenty-three. Maybe you already know those comforting words: "The Lord is my shepherd . . ." (*Let the participants recite the psalm, if appropriate.*) Words that we associate with the loss of those we love bring us peace during difficult times.

Later, however, when we hear those words again, grief may wash back over us like an unexpected wave crashing against the shore and catching us by surprise. The words from the psalm read at the funeral of our loved one can become a "trigger," echoing our grief, like the conch shell's sound makes us think we're at the ocean again.

The triggers, or reminders of grief, come to us in many ways and at various times—the date of a birthday, a favorite color, and a shared memory can all bring back the heartache and emptiness we feel when we think of the one we have lost. However, as the psalmist reminds us, we "walk through" the valley of the shadow of death. We don't stay there. We remember that "goodness and mercy" do follow us as we keep going toward God. And we, like the person whose loss we grieve, will "dwell in the house of the Lord, forever."

PRAYER:
Dear God, Thank you for shepherding us through the valley of the shadow of death. Help us to remember that you will help us with our sadness when we think we can't go on. Amen.

25
River of Life: A Picture of Heaven

HYMN STORY: "Shall We Gather at the River?"

PASSAGE: Revelation 22:1-2

PURPOSE: The river of life represents the pure and perfect source of God's power found in our heavenly home.

PREPARATION: Materials to make a Drawing of Heaven: Crayons; Markers; Music for "Shall We Gather at the River?"; Paper; Pictures of rivers.

METHOD:

Draw a picture of "heaven," including a river, to illustrate the hymn, "Shall We Gather at the River?"

Invite the congregation to sing the hymn before sharing the children's story.

PRESENTATION:

How do you picture heaven? If I gave you crayons or markers and paper, how would you draw the place we call "heaven"? (*Discuss ideas or, if time permits, allow the children to depict and describe their visions of heaven.*) You have wonderful ways of showing what heaven might be like. In the Christian Scriptures, the book of Revelation describes heaven as a place with a beautiful, crystal-clear river. This is a lovely way to picture God's power. (*Hold up an illustration as well as calendar or magazine pictures of landscapes with rivers flowing through them.*) A flowing river creates a scenic view where people would enjoy spending time. In heaven, we will spend eternity enjoying the beauty of God's presence and the joy of being with all those we love.

Sometimes, however, people picture death as a dark and fearful river. One time, during an epidemic when many people were dying, a pastor by the name of Robert Lowry grew very weary of hearing people talk only about the river of death. He wanted to give the people of his church a more positive picture to hold in their minds as they faced life's challenges. He wanted them to remember the River of Life mentioned in the book of Revelation. In his mind he tried to picture the scene described. Reverend Lowry imagined what it would be like to gather with those friends and family who were already with God in heaven. As he contemplated the joyful scene, he sat at the organ in his parlor and thought of the question, "Shall we gather at the river?" In his mind, he imagined a chorus of joyful voices answering that question: "Yes, we'll gather at the river!" Quickly, he was able to write both the words and the music to a hymn that gives a much more positive way of thinking about what comes after death—a celebration of the River of Life that flows to us directly from God.

While we may not know exactly what heaven will look like or exactly where heaven is, we can begin to picture our "heavenly home" and understand that it will be more beautiful and more full of joy than we could ever begin to imagine.

PRAYER:
Dear God, Thank you for giving us an idea of heaven as a beautiful place. Help us to invite others to picture your promise of the River of Life. Amen.

26
Sarah's Death: A Mother's Connection

PASSAGE: Genesis 23:1-2; 24:67

PURPOSE: Sarah's death reminds us that we never forget the connection we have with our mothers.

PREPARATION: Baby Doll (with visible "belly button")

PRESENTATION:

Everyone loves to rock little babies, don't they? (*Rock the baby doll.*) Doesn't this baby doll look real? The manufacturers even gave the baby a "belly button." (*Let the participants see the "belly button."*) Everyone has a "belly button," right? That's because all of us were attached to our mothers with a cord before we were born. That cord nourished us and kept us alive inside of our mothers' bodies until we were ready to breathe and eat on our own. We carry the mark of our attachment to our mothers all our lives.

One of the stories from the Hebrew Scriptures tells of a woman who thought she was never going to become a mother. Her name was Sarah. God had promised Abraham and Sarah that they would have a child. But the story tells us that Sarah was ninety years old before God's promise finally came true. That seems impossible, doesn't it? But the point is that nothing is impossible for God. Isaac was born to Sarah and Abraham. Not only that, Sarah lived to be one hundred twenty seven years old! So Isaac was nearly forty when his mother died. However, no matter how long we live, our mother's death is a time of great loss.

God and other people can comfort us when we lose our mothers; nevertheless, there will always be a place inside our hearts that reminds us of the loss we feel. Just like our "belly buttons" remind us that we were once physically connected, our grief reminds us that we are still connected by love to the person who nurtured us from the very beginning. Death, like birth, is a natural part of life. We can learn to survive without our mothers, but we will always remember them. Those memories and God's great love can keep us connected forever.

PRAYER:
Dear God, Keep us connected to you and to the ones we love forever. Amen.

27
Sin's Seeds: A Brother's Murder

Passage: Genesis 4:1-16

Purpose: Anger is not a sin, but misused anger can lead us to embrace the wrong rather than to follow God's ways.

Preparation: Seeds

Presentation:

Do you know what kind of seeds these are? *(Hold up the seeds.)* If we plant these seeds, what will they produce? *(Allow the participants to respond.)* How do you know? Of course, seeds reproduce the plant they came from, don't they? In early times, most people had to plant their own food to eat and raise their own animals. The very first family—Adam and Eve and their children Cain and Abel—were farmers. Cain grew grain and Abel tended animals. To honor God, each son offered a portion of what he had grown as a sacrifice. The story from Genesis tells us that God preferred Abel's gift—for what reason isn't clear. It could have been that Cain's heart simply was not in the right place. He was envious of his brother and hated him because it seemed God was more pleased with Abel than with Cain.

Of course, God reassured Cain that he could try again. Unfortunately, Cain chose to plant seeds of anger and bitterness, and he received the fruit of the crop he planted. You see, Cain murdered Abel. As a result, he was punished by God and sent away from his family and from God's blessing. Most likely, he never asked for forgiveness or repented of his decision to kill his brother. He also did not choose to seek God's help with the guilt of the choice he had made. Only God can remove the seeds of sin from our lives; we cannot do it without God's help.

How nice it would be if we could say that murder was only something that happened one time, long ago. Sadly, the human race continues to plant seeds of sin and the world suffers the pain and sadness that comes from one human being's violence toward another. All of us experience anger, even jealousy, and bitterness. The important lesson is that we can turn to God for help with those destructive feelings. We must not continue to plant the seeds of sin that destroy. Instead, we may ask God to take away our sin and give us a new heart that loves and values others. So long as we are on earth, there will be sin. But as often as we turn to Christ—and to the people God gives us to help make good choices, we can find forgiveness for sin and plant the seeds that will produce a harvest of hope.

PRAYER:
Dear God, Help us to value each other as your children. Give us your grace to plant seeds that lead to peace. Amen.

28
Stephen's Story: A Martyr's Faith

PASSAGE: Acts 7:54-60

PURPOSE: A martyr's death is a living testimony to a believer's strong faith in God's love.

PREPARATION: Rock

PRESENTATION:

Who knows what this is? (*Hold up a large rock and wait for responses.*) That's right. It's a big rock or a large stone. Have you ever been hit by one of these? (*Wait for answers.*) What do you think might happen if you were? (*Affirm replies.*) That's right, if you were hit by a rock like this you would get hurt. If you were struck hard enough, or if many rocks hit you, you might even die. That is what happened to Stephen, a man we read about in the book of Acts. Stephen was the first Christian martyr. A martyr is a person who dies because of his or her testimony about Jesus' crucifixion and resurrection. Stephen was telling people about God's love and about Jesus' ministry when he was "stoned" to death.

Stephen believed in Jesus and did things that helped many people. He fed those who were hungry and he took care of the sick. And while he was doing these things he told them about Jesus. Of course, the people he helped really liked him, but others were jealous of how popular he had become. So they told lies about him and said very bad things. The people got angry and stoned Stephen. Even while he was dying Stephen talked about Jesus' gift of salvation and about God's love for everyone.

Stephen was the first martyr, but he wasn't the last. Many people died because of their faith when the church was just starting; but even after Christianity had spread all over the world some people were killed because they loved Jesus. Sometimes missionaries are still killed because they tell people about Jesus. Jesus is more important to them than anything else—even their lives on earth.

There are other Christians who are not killed by an angry mob, but who are still martyrs. These are people who suffer a lot from an illness before they die. Other people may say, "Why doesn't God heal you? Maybe your faith isn't strong enough. Or, maybe God doesn't love you enough to make you better." When someone hears this and still trusts in God and loves Jesus right up to the moment they die, they are like Stephen. Nothing can keep them from loving Jesus and from trusting God. Isn't this a wonderful living testimony?

PRAYER:

Dear God, We thank you for the testimony of Stephen's life and death. We thank you for all those who die proclaiming your love. Help us to have faith like that. Amen.

29
Suicide's Shock: Expressing Emotions

C S
U II D E

PASSAGE: Hebrews 4:16

PURPOSE: At the time of a suicide, we must turn to God's Word and to God's people to find ways to express the emotions connected with the death.

PREPARATION: Alphabet Letters—S, U, I, C, I, D, E
(Cut out letters from magazines and newspapers; make them from sponges, stamps, or stencils; or use magnetic letters or printing sets.)

PRESENTATION:
I'd like you to help me use these letters to spell a very difficult word. (*Hold up the letters.*) Let's name each letter before we begin—C, S, E, I, D, I, U. (*Name each letter in random order.*) Any guesses? I told you it was a hard word to spell. Let me give you a hint. The word starts with the letter "S." (*Attempt combinations of letters until the word "Suicide" is formed.*) The word is "Suicide." It's a hard word to spell. It's also a difficult topic to discuss. Suicide is a choice to end one's own life.

At the time of a death, we are often at a loss for words. If the death is a suicide, it is even more difficult to talk about the situation. Some people die because of illnesses of the heart or other organs, many individuals die from cancer, while some others die because their brains or minds are ill with a disease that makes it hard for them to want to live. Families often find it hard to accept that the death of their loved one was by suicide. They prefer to say that the cause was an accident or an illness. In the case of suicide, people search for reasons why someone important to them made such a difficult choice. Many husbands and wives, fathers and mothers, and brothers and sisters ask themselves if there was something they said or something they did that caused the drastic death. And they often come up with words—answers—such as alcohol, change, depression, drugs, and problems. For the family, as well as acquaintances, investigators, and observers, emotions like blame, confusion, denial, guilt, and shame are spoken—and unspoken.

We need to turn to God's Word to find "words" to express our feelings when someone we love chooses to take his or her life. And we need to share these words with others in helpful and hopeful ways. People who find "words" to express their emotions usually feel better than those who try to hide their feelings. We can also turn to God's people, like parents or pastors and doctors or teachers, to help us think about positive words like acceptance, forgiveness, and honor.

God's Word, the Bible, tells us that all of God's children are important to God and are loved by Jesus. Even at a difficult time, we can approach God through prayer and ask for God's comfort.

PRAYER:
Dear God, Even when it is difficult for us to talk about the sad things that happen in life, help us to remember that you are with us in our times of need. Amen.

30

Tragic Accidents: Finding Our Refuge

Passage: Psalm 46

Purpose: God does not promise that we will be free of unexpected trouble; God does promise to be near during difficult times.

Preparation: Triangle-shaped Highway Safety Marker

Presentation:

Do you know what this is used for? (*Hold up triangle-shaped highway safety marker.*) When an emergency occurs on a highway, drivers or members of the highway patrol use these to alert other motorists to watch out for a dangerous situation. Driving past an accident on the highway can be very upsetting, even if we were not a part of what occurred. We don't understand why bad things like fatal accidents suddenly happen to good people. Or we may be troubled when we learn of other accidents in which people fall, drown, or perhaps die from gunshot wounds or poisonous substances. Sometimes our first question is "How could God let something like this happen?" Accidents seem so unfair and catch us by surprise in a way that can shake our faith.

The Bible doesn't tell us why accidents occur. However, the Scriptures promise that God will be with us no matter what happens on earth. Psalm 46 says that even though the earth would come to an end, God would still be with us and be our refuge, our safe place. While it seems impossible not to be afraid of something like the world coming to an end, we can learn not to focus on our fears, but to focus on God's eternal power instead. No matter what happens in this life, God's love and strength will be with us. God hasn't promised that upsetting things won't happen in the lives of believers; God has promised never to leave us or forsake us.

The challenge to us, then, is to learn to put our trust in God's power. Verse ten of Psalm 46 is a good one to memorize so that in times of trouble and distress, we will remember that God says: "Be still and know that I am God." Even as we look at the emergency symbol we can be reminded to keep our focus on God. The triangle is a Christian symbol for the Trinity, the three ways we understand God: as Father or Creator, as Son or Savior, and as Holy Spirit or Ever-present Power. Our faith will see us through whatever unforeseen experience life may bring, with this foundation for our lives.

PRAYER:
Dear God, Help us in times of trouble to turn to you for help. Thank you that you are always near. Amen.

Age-Group Suggestions

Life after death is a central theme of the story of faith. Jesus came to earth to bring eternal life to those who accept God's gift of salvation. Faith in Christ gives us the ability to live in confidence, freed from the fear of death. For Christians, the empty tomb symbolizes the hope of resurrection and God's power to grant everlasting life. It is this hope that enables Christians to face the reality of death. Christ has gone to "prepare a place for us" that we may be forever in God's presence. Therefore, death is not a topic to be avoided by Christians. However, like all of life's experiences, death may be understood on a variety of levels. Parents, pastors, and educators must be sensitive to the participants' readiness to comprehend symbols, rituals, and themes associated with the end of life on earth. Consider the following suggestions to explore topics related to death with different age groups. Use them in a variety of settings and situations that will allow God's people, young and old, to discuss, understand, and reach out in Christian compassion during times of grief and pain.

Preschool: Nature's Cycle

- Display pictures of trees in each season and connect spring's reawakening buds to God's promise of new life in Christ.
- Read the book *Lifetimes: The Beautiful Way to Explain Death to Children* by Bryan Mellonie and Robert R. Ingpen (New York: Bantam Doubleday Dell, 1983) and show the illustrations to help demonstrate the reality that everything that lives must also die.
- Visit a butterfly exhibit or create a display depicting the stages of metamorphosis.

Early Elementary: Bible Stories

◊ Read John 3:16, inserting each child's own name in the place of "the world." Explain that God sent Jesus to bring eternal life to each one of God's children. Help each person commit the text to memory.

◊ Use a children's Bible to retell the story of how death came into the world through the sin of Adam and Eve.

◊ View the story of Jesus' resurrection on an Easter video; then discuss the events, emphasizing Christ's victory over death.

Upper Elementary: Vocabulary

◊ Brainstorm, look up, and write definitions for words that relate to death, like cemetery, coffin, cremation, funeral, hearse, and resurrection.

◊ Construct a banner or collage of terms related to the theme of eternal life.

◊ Create a cooperative picture book to help younger children understand the meaning of resurrection.

Middle School: Interviews

◊ Ask students to interview on audio or video tape a grandparent or an older adult to discover stories about family members who have died; then share these stories with the class.

◊ Invite a funeral director to visit the class to answer questions about how he or she helps families during difficult times.

◊ Write questions to the pastor about concerns or wonderings regarding death and arrange a time for discussion.

High School: Memorials

◊ Plan a special memorial service of All Saints' Day, Veterans' Day, or another local or national commemorative occasion. Select music, readings, and speakers and organize the presentation.

◊ Research some of the history behind memorial gifts in the church building like pew Bibles and stained glass windows. Discover answers to questions such as: Who gave them? When? Why? Present the findings to younger classes or to confirmands.

♦ Visit a cemetery to explore types of memorials on gravestones. Discuss what the sentiments and symbols reveal about the people who have passed away. Have the participants design a memorial they would prefer for themselves.

Adult: Issues

♦ Brainstorm challenging life and death issues that Christians face in today's world: abortion, alternative therapies or treatments for terminal illness, assisted suicide, capital punishment, and war. Invite speakers and plan units of study around one or more topics.

♦ Invite a hospital chaplain to meet with the participants to discuss end-of-life issues such as hospice care, living wills, and visits to the terminally ill.

♦ Visit a funeral home to learn about preplanning of funeral arrangements.

Hymn Story
Cross-References

"For All the Saints"
All Saints' Day: A Cloud of Witnesses

"Hymn of Promise"
Nature's Lesson: New Beginnings

"Precious Lord, Take My Hand"
Faithful Hands: A Grandparent's Death

"Shall We Gather at the River?"
River of Life: A Picture of Heaven

Scripture Cross-References

Old Testament

Genesis 3
>   *Adam and Eve's Sin: Our Redemption*

Genesis 4:1-16
>   *Sin's Seeds: A Brother's Murder*

Genesis 23:1-2; 24:67
>   *Sarah's Death: A Mother's Connection*

Genesis 25:7-10
>   *Abraham's Death: Farewell to a Father*

Joshua 4:4-7
>   *God's Faithfulness: Anniversary Memories*

Job 1:21b
>   *Empty Chair: A Classmate's Death*

Psalm 23
>   *Psalm Twenty-Three: Words of Comfort*

Psalm 46
>   *Tragic Accidents: Finding Our Refuge*

Isaiah 41:13
>   *Faithful Hands: A Grandparent's Death*

Isaiah 43:2-3a
>   *God's Shelter: Facing a Disaster*

Ecclesiastes 3:1-8
>   *Nature's Lesson: New Beginnings*

New Testament

Matthew 27:1-13

Heavenly Bodies: Our Transfiguration

Matthew 27:45-56

Good Friday's Gift: Forgiveness

Matthew 27:57-60

Jesus' Burial: Joseph's Compassion

Matthew 28:1-7

Easter's Promise: Eternal Life

Mark 15:33-41

Good Friday's Gift: Forgiveness

Mark 15:42-46

Jesus' Burial: Joseph's Compassion

Mark 16:1-8

Easter's Promise: Eternal Life

Luke 15:3-7

Jesus' Stories: A Lost Pet

Luke 23:44-49

Good Friday's Gift: Forgiveness

Luke 23:50-53

Jesus' Burial: Joseph's Compassion

Luke 23:55-24:1

Preparation for Burial: Finding Comfort

Luke 24:1-12

Easter's Promise: Eternal Life

John 11:21

Lazarus's Death: Grieving a Sibling

John 14:1-3

Christ's Second Coming: A Comforting Promise

John 14:16

Pentecost's Power: The Holy Spirit's Comfort

John 19:28-37

Good Friday's Gift: Forgiveness

John 19:38-42

Jesus' Burial: Joseph's Compassion

John 20:1-10

Easter's Promise: Eternal Life

Acts 7:54-60

Stephen's Story: A Martyr's Faith

Romans 6:23
> *Christmas's Gift: Sin's Death*

Romans 13:7a, c
> *Memorial Day: Honoring Heroes*

1 Corinthians 13:12
> *Paul's Prophecy: Facing Life's Questions*

1 Corinthians 15:26
> *Epiphany's Message: Jesus' Mission*

1 Corinthians 15:47-49
> *Death's Decisions: Choosing Cremation*

Hebrews 4:16
> *Suicide's Shock: Expressing Emotions*

Hebrews 12:1
> *All Saints' Day: A Cloud of Witnesses*

Revelation 14:13
> *Funeral Service: Final Farewell*

Revelation 22:1-2
> *River of Life: A Picture of Heaven*

Teaching Tool
Cross-References

Alphabet Letters	*Suicide's Shock: Expressing Emotions*
Apple	*Adam and Eve's Sin: Our Redemption*
Baby Doll	*Sarah's Death: A Mother's Connection*
Baby Picture	*Heavenly Bodies: Our Transfiguration*
Bible	*Jesus' Burial: Joseph's Compassion*
Chair	*Empty Chair: A Classmate's Death*
Children's Book—*Wilfrid Gordon McDonald Partridge*	
	God's Faithfulness: Anniversary Memories
Chrismon Ornament	
	Christmas's Gift: Sin's Death
Comforter	*Pentecost's Power: The Holy Spirit's Comfort*
Compass	*Christ's Second Coming: A Comforting Promise*
Conch Shell	*Psalm Twenty-Three: Words of Comfort*
Disaster Kit	*God's Shelter: Facing a Disaster*
Drawing of Heaven	
	River of Life: A Picture of Heaven
Easter Lily Bulb	*Easter's Promise: Eternal Life*
Easter Lily	*Easter's Promise: Eternal Life*
Family Tree Genealogical Chart	
	Abraham's Death: Farewell to a Father
Footsteps	*Lazarus's Death: Grieving a Sibling*
Gifts: Gold, Frankincense, and Myrrh	
	Epiphany's Message: Jesus' Mission
Jar of Earth	*Death's Decisions: Choosing Cremation*
Map	*Christ's Second Coming: A Comforting Promise*

Memorial Card   *Funeral Service: Final Farewell*
Memorial Wreath

                      Memorial Day: Honoring Heroes
Mirror   *Paul's Prophecy: Facing Life's Questions*
Nails   *Good Friday's Gift: Forgiveness*
Picture Frame (Cloud)

                      All Saints' Day: A Cloud of Witnesses
Pictures of Rivers   *River of Life: A Picture of Heaven*
Rock   *Stephen's Story: A Martyr's Faith*
Seeds   *Sin's Seeds: A Brother's Murder*
Shepherd's Crook

                      Jesus' Stories: A Lost Pet
Triangle-shaped Highway Safety Marker

                      Tragic Accidents: Finding Our Refuge
Travel Kit   *Preparation for Burial: Finding Comfort*
Two-part Puzzles   *Nature's Lesson: New Beginnings*
Work Glove   *Faithful Hands: A Grandparent's Death*
Yellow Pages Phone Book

                      Jesus' Burial: Joseph's Compassion

Theme
Cross-References

Church Year

ADVENT
Adam and Eve's Sin: Our Redemption

CHRISTMAS
Christmas's Gift: Sin's Death

EASTER
Easter's Promise: Eternal Life

EPIPHANY
Epiphany's Message: Jesus' Mission

GOOD FRIDAY
Good Friday's Gift: Forgiveness

ORDINARY TIME
Nature's Lesson: New Beginnings

PENTECOST
Pentecost's Power: The Holy Spirit's Comfort

Hymn Stories

"For All the Saints"
All Saints' Day: A Cloud of Witnesses

"Precious Lord, Take My Hand"
Faithful Hands: A Grandparent's Death

"Hymn of Promise"
Nature's Lesson: New Beginnings

"Shall We Gather at the River?"
River of Life: A Picture of Heaven

Scripture/Theology

COMFORT
Pentecost's Power: The Holy Spirit's Comfort
Psalm Twenty-Three: Words of Comfort

DEATH/SIN
Adam and Eve's Sin: Our Redemption

ETERNAL LIFE
Christmas's Gift: Sin's Death
Easter's Promise: Eternal Life
Nature's Lesson: New Beginnings

FORGIVENESS
Adam and Eve's Sin: Our Redemption
Christmas's Gift: Sin's Death
Good Friday's Gift: Forgiveness

HEAVEN
Heavenly Bodies: Our Transfiguration
River of Life: A Picture of Heaven

JESUS' DEATH
Adam and Eve's Sin: Our Redemption
Christmas's Gift: Sin's Death
Epiphany's Message: Jesus' Mission

Good Friday's Gift: Forgiveness
Jesus' Burial: Joseph's Compassion
Preparation for Burial: Finding Comfort

PHYSICAL/SPIRITUAL BODIES
Heavenly Bodies: Our Transfiguration

SECOND COMING
Christ's Second Coming: A Comforting Promise

Special Days

ALL SAINTS' DAY
All Saints' Day: A Cloud of Witnesses

ANNIVERSARY OF DEATH
God's Faithfulness: Anniversary Memories

MEMORIAL DAY
Memorial Day: Honoring Heroes

Specific Deaths - People

DEATH OF A CHILD
Empty Chair: A Classmate's Death

DEATH OF A CLASSMATE
Empty Chair: A Classmate's Death

DEATH OF A FATHER
Abraham's Death: Farewell to a Father

DEATH OF A FRIEND
Empty Chair: A Classmate's Death

DEATH OF A GRANDPARENT
Faithful Hands: A Grandparent's Death

DEATH OF A MOTHER
Sarah's Death: A Mother's Connection

CREMATION
Death's Decisions: Choosing Cremation
Jesus' Burial: Joseph's Compassion

FUNERAL
Funeral Service: Final Farewell
Jesus' Burial: Joseph's Compassion
Preparation for Burial: Finding Comfort

GRAVESIDE
Preparation for Burial: Finding Comfort

GRIEF
Lazarus's Death: Grieving a Sibling
Psalm Twenty-Three: Words of Comfort

LIFE CYCLE/NATURE
Death's Decisions: Choosing Cremation
Nature's Lesson: New Beginnings

MEMORIAL SERVICE
Funeral Service: Final Farewell
Jesus' Burial: Joseph's Compassion

MEMORIES
God's Faithfulness: Anniversary Memories

VIEWING/VISITATION/WAKE
Funeral Service: Final Farewell
Jesus' Burial: Joseph's Compassion
Preparation for Burial: Finding Comfort

About the Authors

Phyllis Vos Wezeman

Phyllis Vos Wezeman is President of Active Learning Associates, Inc., and Director of Christian Nurture at First Presbyterian Church in South Bend, Indiana. Phyllis has served as Adjunct Faculty in the Education Department at Indiana University and the Department of Theology at the University of Notre Dame. She has taught at the Saint Petersburg (Russia) State University and the Shanghai (China) Teacher's University. Phyllis, who holds an M.S. in Education from Indiana University, is a recipient of three "Distinguished Alumna Awards" and the Catholic Library Association's Aggiornamento Award. Author or coauthor of over 900 books and articles, Phyllis and her husband, Ken, have three children and three grandsons.

Anna L. Liechty

Anna Liechty is a National Board Certified teacher and chair of the English Department at Plymouth High School in Indiana. She has also worked as a Religious Education volunteer, teaching all levels, directing Sunday morning and youth programming, consulting with congregations about their educational ministry, and writing a wide variety of religious education materials. She serves as Vice President of Active Learning Associates, Inc. Anna lives in Plymouth, Indiana, with her husband, Ron, a retired pastor. They have five children and ten grandchildren.

Kenneth R. Wezeman

Ken holds an M.Div. from Calvin Theological Seminary, Grand Rapids, Michigan, and has served as a chaplain at Ypsilanti State Hospital (MI), Georgia Mental Health Institute (GA), Appalachian Regional Hospitals (KY), Osteopathic Hospital (IN), and Saint Joseph Hospital (IN), as well as a pastor, counselor, and teacher. Ken is currently the Business Manager/Editor of Active Learning Associates, Inc., and the Resource Coordinator of <rotation.org>, the Web site of the Workshop Rotation Model of Christian Education. Coauthor of several books and articles, Ken and his wife, Phyllis, have three children and three grandsons.

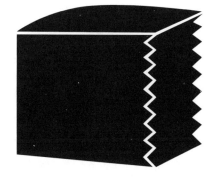

OTHER BOOKS FROM THE PILGRIM PRESS

TASTE THE BREAD
30 Children's Sermons on Communion
Phyllis Vos Wezeman, Anna L. Liechty, and Kenneth R. Wezeman
ISBN 0–8298–1519–8/paper/96 pages/$10.00

TOUCH THE WATER
30 Children's Sermons on Baptism
Phyllis Vos Wezeman, Anna L. Liechty, and Kenneth R. Wezeman
ISBN 0–8298–1518–X/paper/96 pages/$10.00

PLANTING SEEDS OF FAITH
Virginia H. Loewen
ISBN 0–8298–1473–6/paper/96 pages/$10.00

GROWING SEEDS OF FAITH
Virginia H. Loewen
ISBN 0–8298–1488–4/paper/96 pages/$10.00

THE BROWN BAG
Jerry Marshall Jordan
ISBN 0–8298–0411–0/paper/117 pages/$9.95

SMALL WONDERS
Sermons for Children
Glen E. Rainsley
ISBN 0–8298–1252–0/paper/104 pages/$12.95

TIME WITH OUR CHILDREN
Stories for Use in Worship, Year B
Dianne E. Deming
ISBN 0–8298–0952–X/paper/182 pages/$9.95

TIME WITH OUR CHILDREN
Stories for Use in Worship, Year C
Dianne E. Deming
ISBN 0–8298–0953–8/paper/157 pages/$9.95

To order these or any other books from The Pilgrim Press, call or write to:
The Pilgrim Press
700 Prospect Avenue East
Cleveland, Ohio 44115–1100
Phone orders: 800.537.3394
Fax orders: 216.736.2206
Please include shipping charges of $4.00 for the first book and 75¢ for each additional book.
Or order from our Web sites, <www.pilgrimpress.com> and <www.ucpress.com>.
Prices subject to change without notice.